My Tired Brain

A Child's Journey to Understanding
Sleep Apnea

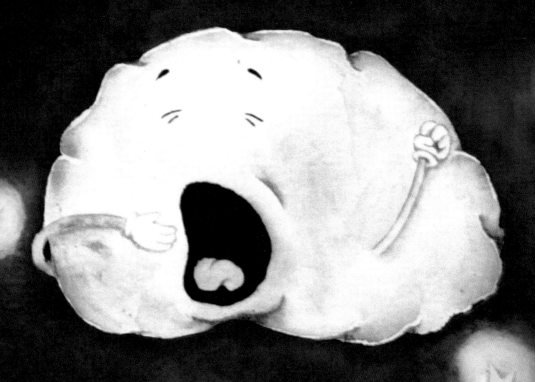

By Angela Deal

Illustrated by Brandon Smith

Dedication

On behalf of children diagnosed with pediatric sleep apnea:
I dedicate this book to you.

To my youngest son, Gavin: I have been inspired by you to match your courage and "no quit" attitude as I try my hand at writing. I am hoping that what we have learned together about sleep apnea will shed light and provide support for other families.

To my other two children, Madeline and Jason, who would be upset if I didn't mention them: Thank you for your ongoing support and enthusiasm.

Finally, to my husband, Steve, who didn't laugh when I told him about this idea to write a book: I could not have done this without your support.

This project would not have been completed without the support from Summit Pointe/Behavioral Health Resources, Battle Creek Center for Sleep Health, Anne Perry Photography, and the children who volunteered to be photographed.

Thank You

My brain is cool!
It helps me to run fast,
jump high,
think smart,
and share my feelings well.
Our brains work best when they get
a good night's sleep!

Unfortunately, MY brain is tired and sleepy most days. When it's tired, I am grumpy and cranky. I have a hard time listening and I don't do what my mom and dad ask.

Sometimes I cry because my brother ate the last of my favorite cereal. I also get angry when I can't double knot my shoe laces. It takes me a long time to calm down.

I feel sad when I have those feelings.

My brain is tired because it doesn't get enough sleep at night. I try to go to bed early and take extra naps, but it doesn't work.

If I had special ears, I'm sure I could hear my brain *yaaawning* all day long!

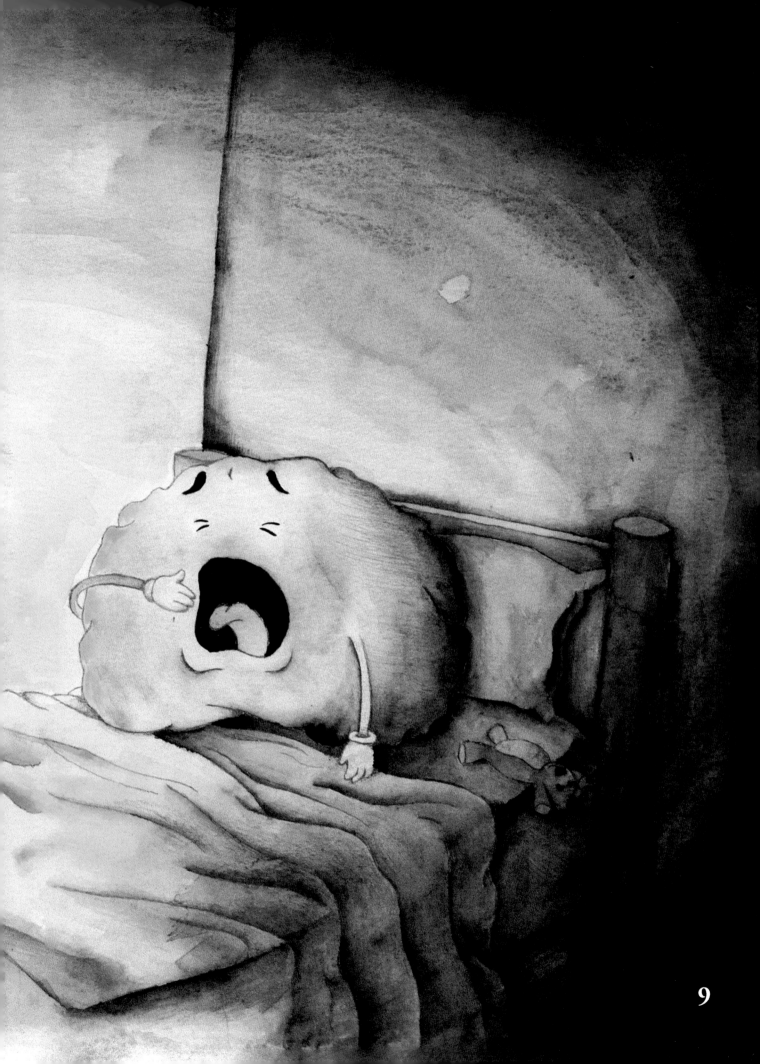

One day, my parents took me to a special doctor who wanted to help my tired brain. This was a very different kind of doctor's appointment. Instead of looking inside my ears or throat, she was going to watch me sleep at night! They called this a *sleep study* and it scared me because I had never done this before.

My mom told me I would be less scared if I brought my favorite things. I grabbed my baseball pj's, my blankie and my teddy bear and shoved them in my backpack. When we got to the sleep study the room looked like a hotel. There was a comfy bed, a bathroom and even a TV! Mom said we were pretending to be on a special trip.

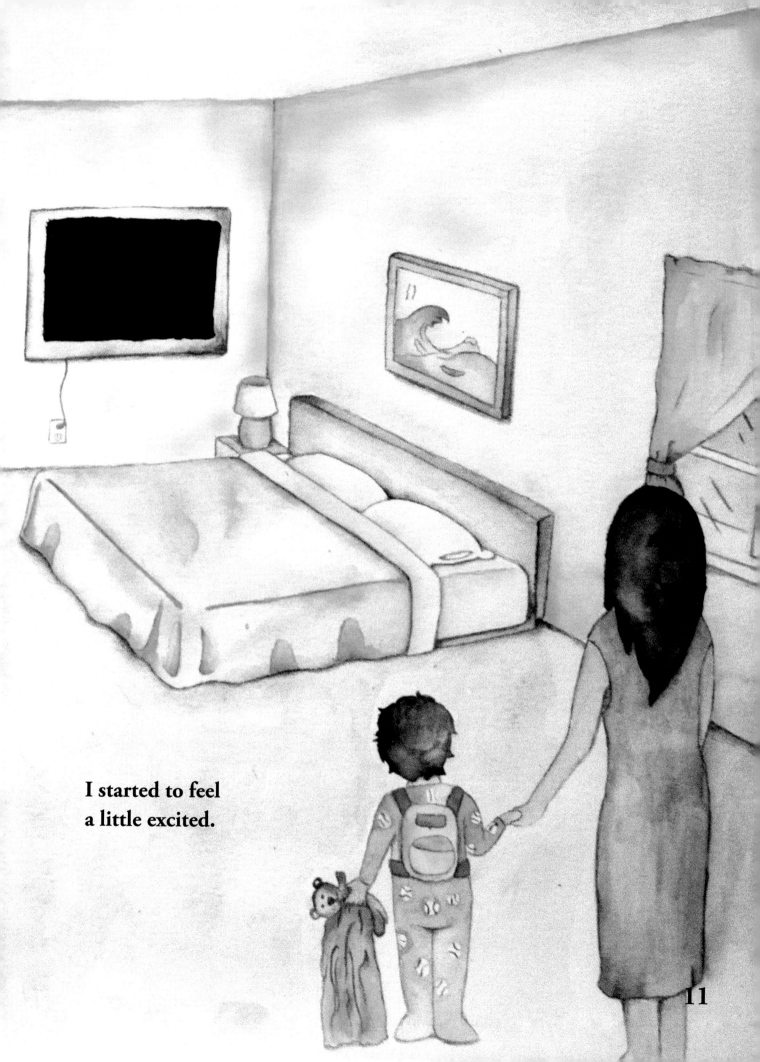

I started to feel
a little excited.

11

The doctor's job was to learn what my body does while I'm sleeping. Watching me sleep gave her clues as to why my brain is so tired. She also used her extra special computer to solve this mystery. The computer was super smart and used special wires to talk with my body. My body told the wires all about my breathing and the number of times my brain woke up while I slept. I told you it was a smart computer!

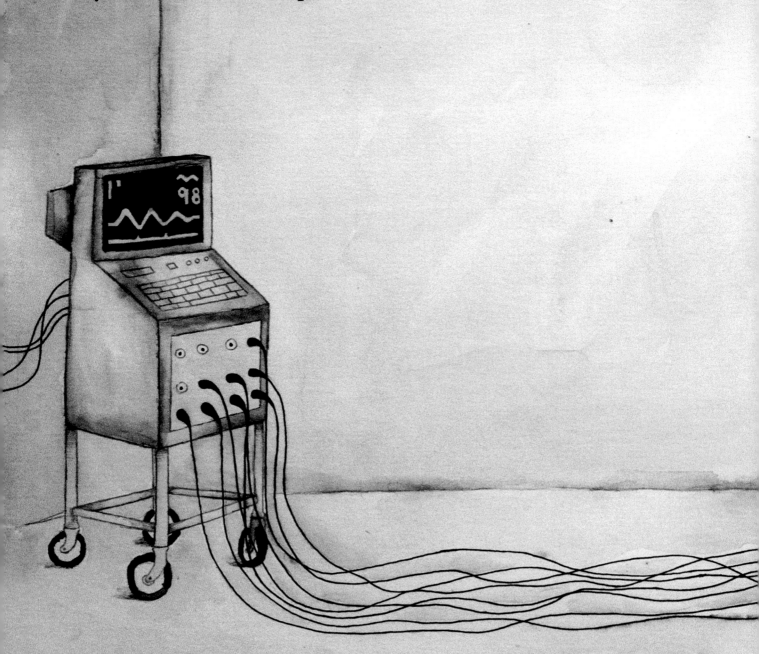

To get me ready to go to sleep, the doctor spent a long time sticking those wires to my body. They were on my face, my chest, my legs and even in my hair! To help them stick better the doctor used gooey-goopy-goo. It felt a little cold, but did not hurt a bit!

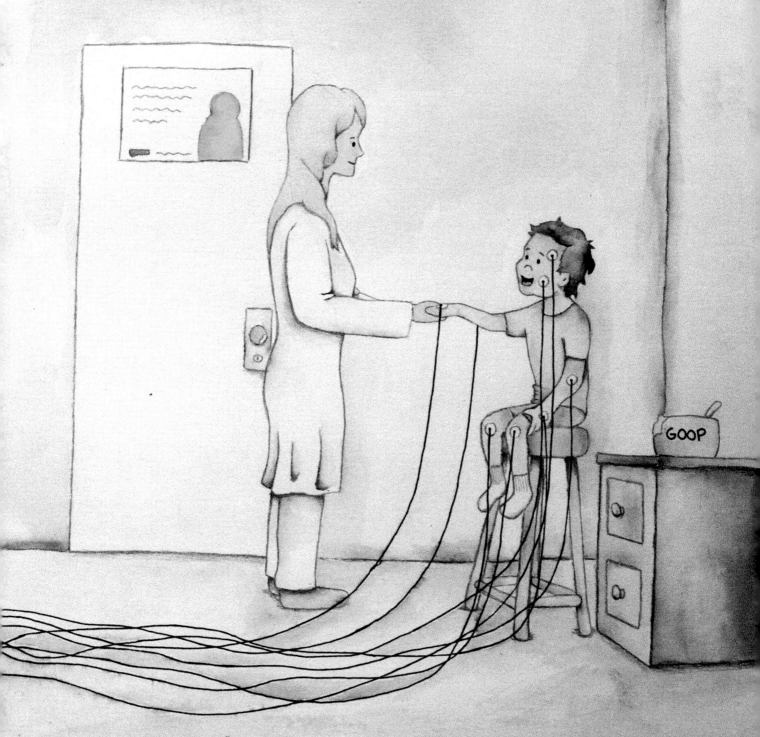

When she finished, I had changed into a robot. I walked around the room with straight legs and stiff arms repeating,

"I-AM-A-BOUT-TO-GO-TO-SLEEP!"

Even my mom jumped up and copied my robot voice saying,

"YOU-ARE-THE-COOL-EST-RO-BOT!"

During the night, the doctor learned that I have something called *sleep apnea*. When I sleep, my lungs will hold their breath. That makes my brain scared, so, it wakes up and shouts to my lungs, "BREATHE!" This surprises my lungs and they take a long, deep breath which makes my brain happy again. My brain will go back to sleep until my lungs decide to hold their breath again. My brain has to wake up and yell at my lungs all night long, so it does not get a good night's sleep.

Now I know why my brain is so *tired* the next day.

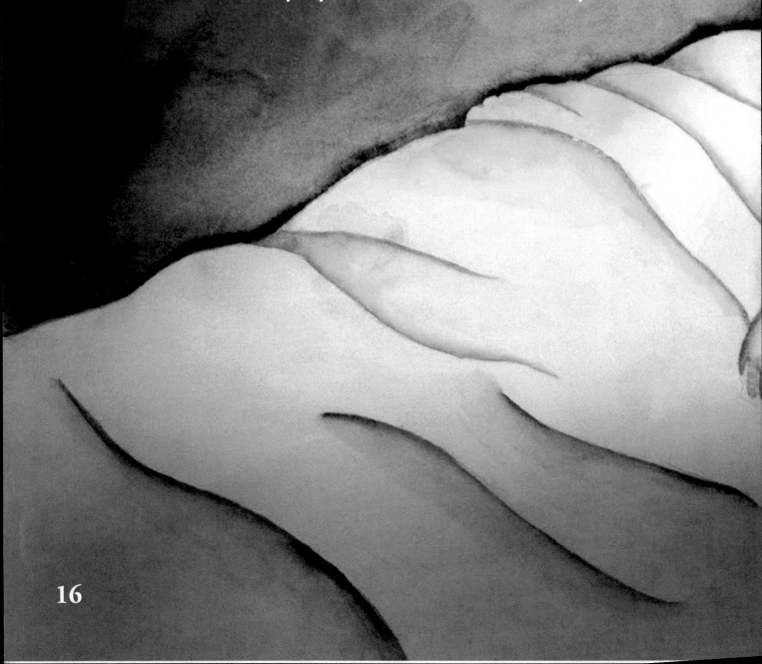

There are a few things doctors can do to help you with sleep apnea. Some kids meet with another special doctor who takes out your tonsils and adenoids. Tonsils and adenoids are located inside your throat. When they become too large they get in the way of breathing. Taking them out helps you breathe better which helps you sleep better!

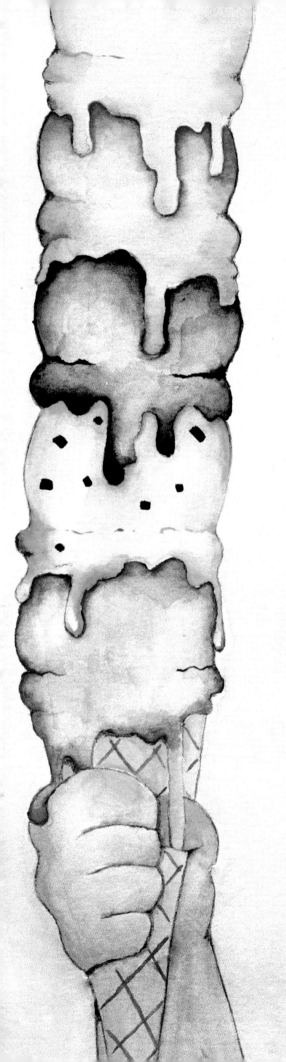

If you have them taken out, your parents might give you a special treat!

Yummmmm!

19

Other kids, like me, get to use a special machine called a CPAP. It's easy to say, just put the words *see* and *pap* together! A CPAP is a small and quiet machine that helps my lungs to breathe while I sleep. When I use my CPAP, I wear a special mask over my nose and mouth. A long tube connects from my mask to the machine. Gentle air travels through the tube and into my nose and mouth at night. This air stops my lungs from holding their breath while I'm asleep. This makes my brain very happy because it can keep on sleeping!

I've seen a CPAP machine before because my dad sleeps with one, too!

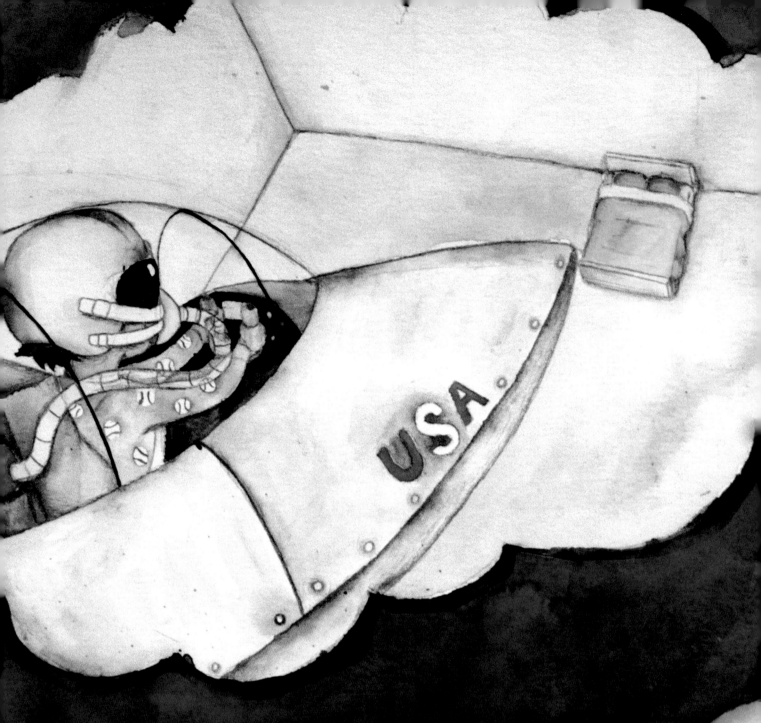

Sometimes, I'll put my mask on and pretend I'm a jet pilot flying through the sky. I hold my arms out strong, fly across my carpet, and land steadily on my bed.

Other nights, I stomp around the room like an elephant, pretending the long tube of the CPAP is my trunk. I tease my older brother, "Watch out, or I'll spray you with water!"

All this silliness helps me to like my mask more.

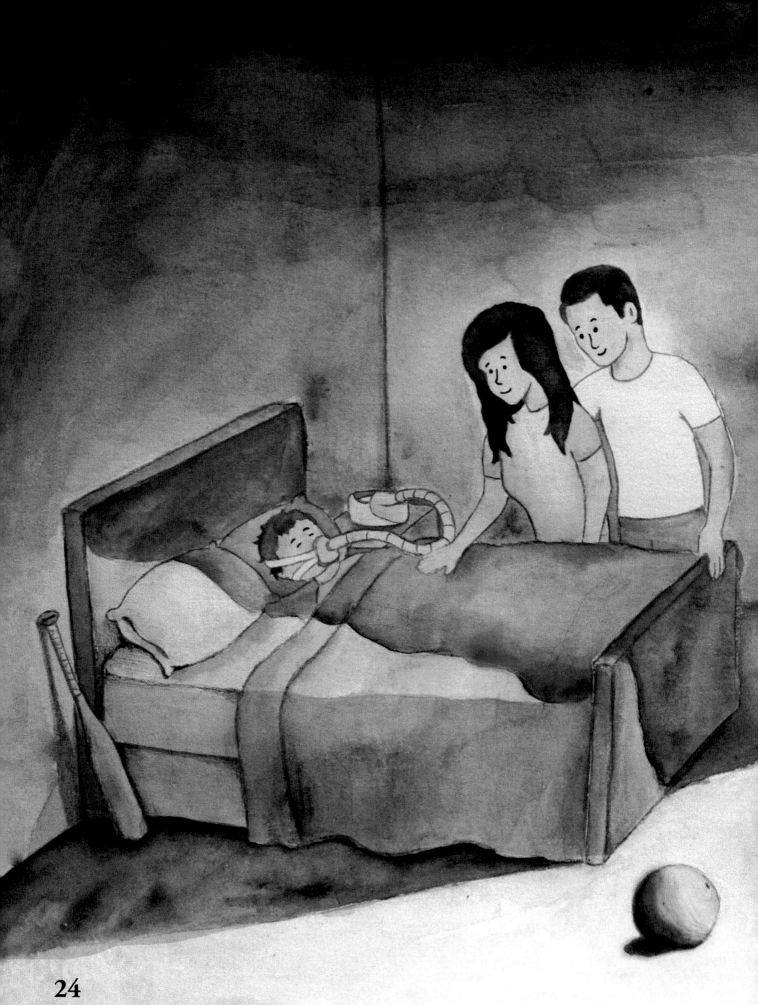

It took a lot of practice to keep my mask on at night because I wasn't used to having something on my face while I slept! Sometimes, I wanted to take it off and not put it back on. But I remember that wearing my mask helps my brain to get a good night's sleep, so I try again. My parents are a big help, too. My mom and dad check on me while I'm sleeping to see if I need any help with my mask. After a lot of practice, I'm finally getting used to wearing it!

I know they are *sooooo* proud of me and give me lots of hugs to show it!

I have been using my CPAP machine for a while now. I am not as cranky or grumpy as before. My ears do a better job at listening, and I feel happier in the morning! Best of all, I don't have to take naps anymore!

I know my brain is smiling because it gets a *gooooood* night's sleep!

Ensuring a Successful Sleep Study

Preparing your child for the sleep study is an important activity. In order to reduce your child's fear and increase his or her chance for a successful sleep study, it is important to take the lead to educate and prepare your child for what to expect. The following suggestions may help you to do just that:

1. Be open and honest about the details of a sleep study. Talk to your child in a patient, calm voice and explain to your child the purpose of each step. Be sure to describe each step at a level he or she can understand.

2. Create a list of questions your child may have about the sleep study and call the physician together to obtain the answers.

3. Use your imagination to find a way to recreate the experience for your child in a safe and positive way. For example, tape yarn on the same parts of the body where the sleep specialist will place the wires. Or have your child role-play this activity by using a favorite doll or stuffed animal.

4. Validate your child's feelings of uneasiness, worry, or fear. Remind her of the importance of sharing her feelings, and be sure to find ways to reduce her anxiety.

5. Keep your emotions under control. Appear calm and relaxed even when your child may become more nervous or reluctant. Always be positive and reassuring!

6. Be sure to recognize your child's efforts and reward him for a job well done!

Mastering the Use of a CPAP

Helping your child become comfortable using a CPAP machine takes a great deal of commitment and patience. Stay focused on how the CPAP machine will greatly benefit your child, and use the following suggestions to reach the finish line successfully:

1. Be patient, be consistent and be positive.

2. Set realistic expectations regarding the speed your child becomes used to wearing the mask. Think of this experience as training for a marathon rather than a quick sprint.

3. Expect difficult nights when your child may be resistant to wearing the mask. Address those moments with patience and encouragement, and remind yourself that you'll have another opportunity the following night.

4. Set small and reachable goals for your child to obtain. Create a visual chart for your child to view her progress, and identify small rewards that recognize her efforts and accomplishments.

5. Encourage your child to practice wearing the mask while he is awake. This will increase his level of comfort and help to make the mask feel normal.

6. Set your own alarm to check on your child periodically throughout the night. Identify any patterns with how your child uses the mask, and quickly solve problems if they occur.

7. Don't measure success or failure in terms of one night. Instead, look back over longer periods of one, three and six months to measure your child's progress.

8. Finally, recognize your own efforts in helping your child, and give yourself permission to relax and take a break at times.

Made in United States
Orlando, FL
15 August 2022